THE MAN
BEFORE THE
MILLIONAIRE

By

Pierre McCoy

ISBN

Hardcover: 979-8-90190-362-9

Paperback: 979-8-90190-361-2

I want to dedicate this book to all the children, all the adults, all the teenagers who will one day partake on the Journey of the UNKNOWN. The journey where you stop choosing to follow societal norms or generational curses & you take a path that is not often taken but takes you to a place most people never make it to & that's PURPOSE. Walking toward a side of you that you have never been aware of is difficult. I would say so myself, but the dividends, the outcome, the reward received in the end, if we make it. It is unlike any accomplishment we would ever experience in our lives. Because there is no greater fulfillment, no greater feelings, no greater bliss, than the one you receive from finding your Identity & Purpose in God.

I also want to dedicate this book to my daughters, Kataleya & Loyalty. I love you both so much. Daddy is not perfect, but I want you both to live in creation & Imagination & faith just as Daddy did. Never lose faith in the possibility of abundance & generational change; Cause that is all Daddy ever strived for on this Entrepreneurial Journey of the Unknown. You two are my reasons. You two are my true Why!

Daddy hopes one day you two will get the opportunity to read daddies creation. I also believe that one day you two will create something of your own to give to this world & help other people as well. I love You Both!

Thank you, Kiarra. I could never repay you for this opportunity.

Table of Contents

Introduction

I have never been the most likable person, but I've always remained myself. I have always stayed focused on discovering things about myself I never knew before. If life has taught me anything thus far, it is that you lose possessions and people every day; however, whether you lose yourself in the process is your choice alone.

I have always had trouble being liked. It was unintentional, and most of the time, the trouble was not with women but with men. When I was a little kid, my mom told me that I had taken a daycare teacher's keys that were left outside and driven her car into a tree. She chose not to kick me out. My older sister told me that the same daycare teacher took me to the barbershop without my mom's permission and cut all my hair off. She thought it was too long for me to be a boy. My sister said my mom cried about my hair being cut, but she forgave the daycare teacher just as she forgave me for crashing the van. It was a different situation with the same outcome, all done out of love for me.

Schooling and Struggles

When I was in elementary school, I can remember not having a care in the world. My mom would be called constantly, and I was always being sent home or suspended. I never cared, and I never understood why. In about fourth or fifth grade, I started at a school called St. Marcus. Things got even worse. At St. Marcus, they had strikes; if you got three strikes, you were out! Rather than being struck out like in baseball, you were expelled from middle school.

In middle school, I actually started being attracted to girls, but my way of making them attracted to me was to always have all the attention on me. No matter what. At St. Marcus, I quickly racked up strikes. I was disliked by multiple teachers, no matter how much my mom pleaded. I had two strikes, and with my next strike, I would be out. I had a problem, and my mom was not giving me medication because she had faith in God. She loved me and believed I would get better.

One day at lunch, despite knowing about my strikes and trying to be good, a girl who liked me thought it would be a good time to let me know. She let me know she liked me by throwing peas at my head during silent lunch. I held my patience for as long as I could. Finally, I had had enough and yelled, "Stop, Hannah, before I slap the white off of you!"

I got my third strike and was expelled by the principal, Henry Tyson. Of course, I was not going to slap her, but the statement was strong enough.

After being expelled from St. Marcus, I attended Siloah. I lasted at Siloah for a little while before being expelled from that school as well. I was expelled because it was similar to St. Marcus and also had strikes. As I said, I have always had a problem with being liked, mostly by men.

My first strike at Siloah came while walking up the stairs after the class, wanting to grab some lunch. A little guy wanted to prove himself, I guess, so he walked past my tray and just took the spork off my plate. Everyone began to laugh; maybe it was a joke to them. I knocked his plate out of his hand while dropping mine, and I hit him. My second strike occurred while in class. A guy tried to bully me with a statement he made to the whole class. Again, everyone laughed. I walked up to him and "Sweet Chin Musiced" him right in the chin. The "Sweet Chin Music" is the special finisher move of wrestler Shawn Michaels.

I did it to the guy, and I was kicked out of Siloah.

The Turning Point

After being kicked out of Siloah, I attended Hope Prima. This is the school that changed everything for me. At this school, literally all I did was be the class clown. I did not do any work. I was in the sixth grade, and my sole reason for coming to school was to talk with girls and be a clown. Finally, the year was up, and it was time for everyone to head home for the summer.

Before the teacher let everyone leave for the bus, she stated, "Inside this envelope you are about to receive is the last report card stating if you are moving on to the 7th grade or staying behind." After she stated that, she let everyone leave. I got on the bus with all my friends, and all of them were yelling, "I passed! I moved on!"

One of my friends asked, "Pierre, what does yours say?"

I sat down in my seat and opened my envelope. To my surprise, the paper stated "REPEAT" in big red letters. I told my friends I had moved on, and I sat quietly for my entire ride home. That was the first time in my life I had ever felt embarrassed. Out of all those things I did for which people judged me, I had never felt more embarrassed than having to repeat a grade, knowing it was because I did not try at all. I changed after this, and I was never the same Pierre again.

After failing the 6th grade, I attended Hope Fortis, where I thrived. Yes, I thrived without ever having to take medication. Failing 6th grade was the only switch I needed to flick to change the path I was going down. I had a little trouble at the beginning, but I met two female teachers at Hope Fortis who never gave up on me: Chelsea Procknow and Ms. Huff. They are the reasons I made it through to the eighth grade and graduated from Hope Fortis.

I believe the challenge many kids and adults face with ADHD, which is what I had, should not be treated with medication alone, but with a life-changing moment or people who truly care to not see them fail. In my case, God allowed me both. I believe everyone with a "magical power" similar to mine, like ADHD, should have that option before medication, especially if it is a challenge their parents must deal with, similar to what my mom had to do.

The Magical Power of ADHD

Although I graduated from Hope Fortis, I had an encounter with a teacher in sixth grade that I will never forget. During my second go-around in sixth grade at Hope Fortis, my accelerated math teacher, Mr. Madison, told me that when I got older, I was not going to be very liked. I never believed him until I began my journey of really understanding life. I started to realize I was a loner; I was a loner by choice because while all the guys were grouping up, cracking jokes, and chasing girls, I was deep in thought about whatever was on my mind at the time.

Scientists like to call what I have ADHD, but I call it a magical power. Doctors and scientists believe that is the reason I got expelled from three schools in two years. My mind always runs rapidly. I turn my thoughts into actions quickly, sometimes without making out the difference between a bad and a good thought, but since I was a kid, I've learned to control it. **I learned to control my magical power and my mind. No one thought that I would ever be good; I always got in trouble.** None of my mom's friends wanted to babysit me as a kid, not even our immediate family. Everyone thought Pierre would be the problem child. **No one believed I would turn out how I have today; no one did but my mom and God.**

I always knew I was special, and I always knew I would eventually have control of my thoughts. It took a while, but I learned later on in life that God has not given people many things that they control in this world; but the things we can control, our minds and our choices, make up our perceptions and our positions in life.

The Shift from Worker to Thinker

For example, I used to have an employee mindset until I met with a guy at the University of Wisconsin-Stevens Point, where I eventually attended college, who taught me about the Cashflow Quadrant. Only the sight of it took my mind from thinking I was in school to chase a great, high-paying job to knowing that, rather than working a high-paying job, I could create high-paying jobs for those who did not want to THINK but wanted to WORK.

In this book, I will speak of ways to tackle challenges that life throws at you. **Challenges that you cannot dodge and that you cannot run away from.** I will also speak about the challenges I have had and overcame being me, starting a self-employed business, and having a dream and keeping it from going away. After reading this book, you will not only tackle these challenges, but the doubt you have surrounding these challenges, yourself, and your dream will switch to high faith. You will destroy any challenge you encounter, as well as master yourself, and chase your dream.

Chapter One:
Jobs

When I was younger, my mom, my sisters, and I struggled financially. We did not have much, but my mom always made it happen for us, always. We were a low-middle-class family. I had realized early on that if I wanted expensive things, I was going to have to find a way to get them because my mom could not afford them. My mom could not afford it, but rather than just not affording it, my mom would spend her last on the appearance of my sisters and me, and to make sure we were happy. Most times, I knew she was not happy with the way things were. There were days when we went without lights, heat, or gas, but my mom did her best. I appreciate my mom to this day for everything she has done for me. I only wish she had done more for herself while we were growing up.

My dad was a big-time illegal entrepreneur, a very successful one at that, but I knew deep down that even though he had any luxury car you could name, from Mercedes-Benz to Cadillac and even Hummers, that I did not want to acquire my wealth in the way that he did. My dad was my idol in a lot of ways. I just decided to find my own way to be a young entrepreneur.

My dad was also the flexing type. I did not mind his flexing; what I did not like about his flexing was that he had thousand-dollar outfits on, but sometimes my sister and I would have to beg him for $50. Our moms would often have to call and scream at him for him to pay for something we wanted or to give us extra money to do something. So, I never liked the fact that he flexed in front of people, but behind closed doors, he would penny-pinch with his children.

As things progressed, I got over it, though. To make something of myself, I started young, going door-to-door, finding things, and ways to acquire money. I was very big on yard work because my mom never wanted me in people's houses. So this was the perfect job where I could work and be safe at the same time. I was such a huge networker so young that the people I was working for could not help but get to know me and bring me into their homes because of how comfortable I made them.

One huge message someone should get from reading this chapter is that I have always created a job. **It took me being willing to open up the book I call "MYSELF" to other people so I could have experiences to fill my pages with.** In life, you might think your family has your best interests; but on my journey thus far, I have learned that someone you meet on the street today could care more about your dreams than a family member you've known your entire life.

Never be afraid to be vulnerable; it opens up the path to new conversations.

New Conversation = New Collaboration.

As I spoke about earlier in the chapter, the jobs I created were yard work, picking weeds, and taking out people's trash, sometimes even just talking with them, but they were mine. I say "mine," meaning all income flowing in, I got to decide what happened with it.

I need you to know, as you read this book, that you can be a worker or a thinker. The choice is yours. What I am doing by writing this book is letting you know from my experience that the thinker is the better choice for you and your family. **God has given you a gift, a gift that will make room for you. Much more room than a job you are just doing to get by will ever do.**

The first job I ever had, which I did not own, was at Little Caesars. It showed me that even though I was getting a paycheck, it wasn't mine. Even though I was working hours, they were not my hours. Even though I was very helpful and persistent in becoming a better pizza man, it never made me better. It never made me strong-minded. It never taught me how to file taxes, how to communicate with people, or how to sell myself. It taught me how to sell pizzas.

It also lowered my self-esteem because I was the only guy always working around a ton of women. Women, now and then, want a man with a higher position, not someone working at the same place as them. All Little Caesars gave me was money from the owner's pocket to pay my bills. When I say getting a paycheck from another business isn't your paycheck, I mean it has your name on it, but it also has the name of the company and the man who really owns that check. How will you ever know what it's like to be your own paycheck if someone is always controlling yours?

The second job I ever had, which I did not own, was at Abercrombie & Fitch, a very popular clothing store worldwide. I enjoyed Abercrombie & Fitch, not because it paid well or because I liked my job, but because I got to see and meet people who set a standard of elegance. I also got to meet a ton of girls, so as a young adult, that was a plus. The environment was better, but it was very similar to Little Caesars. I never felt pushed or like I was excelling in life. I felt like I was placing bricks up, but every time I would place a brick, it was gone when I looked back.

I used these jobs as examples because after I stopped working for them, I never wanted to work for anyone else again. Abercrombie & Fitch allowed me the opportunity to network with multiple people while behind their register. It was benefiting me because I was getting better at talking with different kinds of people at a fast pace, but it was benefiting the company much more. **The biggest lesson I learned there about a job is that you truly do not matter. You are as expendable as a baby dropping his fruit on the floor and his parents replacing it with fresher fruit.** I also realized that jobs like to change up their teams; similar to professional sports, jobs will have a great winning team and still look for new "draft picks" (workers).

A job, from my experience, is the thing that will push your dreams so far away from reach that when you finally quit and attempt to reach for your dream, you will forget what your dream was. A job gives the owner of that business power and stability, while you and I just receive a paycheck or a pension. What if you were the one dishing out the paychecks and the petitions? Have you ever imagined what that would be like? Have you ever wondered what it would be like to be the person with the power and stability?

I had another job while working at Abercrombie & Fitch; I was a support teacher at Hope Prima. This was the same school where I failed sixth grade. The same school that changed my life. I plan to be a life coach and a personal development speaker. I thought I wanted to be a teacher, but I realized, working at Hope Prima, that I did not want to be that type of teacher. **While working there, I watched teachers teach who had no plan of their own to help the students; they were just following a curriculum. It was a curriculum that they had no clue if the child was really learning or not.** I always wondered: Does passing a test show that a child is actually learning?

No. Does passing a test show the value of a child's brain? No. I made that one reason why I could not be a teacher and why I disliked jobs.

Should you and I be held accountable for the values of a company that are not our values? Yes, because you and I work for them. Should a teacher be yelled at by a parent whose child is not learning, even if it is a curriculum that they did not create? Yes, because that teacher chose to work for the school. I began to have a whole lot of questions, and ultimately, I left the support teacher role as well. I could not sit around and watch these students learning things that would not propel them in life. I wanted to propel myself in life, and I also wanted to help those kids propel themselves in life. Being a teacher at a school would not allow me to do that. I wanted to control my teachings and the way I went about nurturing kids into their true value.

Not long after, I left Abercrombie & Fitch and was out of a job for a while until I discovered Starbucks. It was close to my home, and after researching it, it seemed like a good, simple job. I applied and got the interview, and they told me they would hire me on the spot. I really got the interview because, after I applied, I called every day until the manager finally said I could come in. I was persistent. I actually wanted to work for Starbucks, and I did.

Starbucks was the fourth job I ever had, which I did not own. Starbucks rewards its employees with stock after a certain period of time dedicated to the company. The Starbucks experience is a great one, in my opinion. Everyone is mostly very nice there. It is a team-based position, similar to being a well-oiled machine. I would compare it to a watch. Everyone has to do their job, or something will fail and ruin the complete rhythm of the process. Starbucks had huge customer loyalty, which was and still is really intriguing to me. I saw similar customers every week. They, in turn, started to remember my face, my name, and even the position I played regularly.

Starbucks makes it hard for an employee to leave, considering they treat their workers so well. You even get weekly tips along with your pay, like it is a restaurant, which Starbucks is not. I enjoyed it, but around this time, my dreams were different.

I was in school at Wisconsin Lutheran College, and I was reading a book called *Before You Quit Your Job* by Robert Kiyosaki. I had never planned to keep working at Starbucks, and after reading that book, I definitely did not.

After hearing what Mou's friend said in that meeting, I never wanted to work a job again. I wanted to own one. I wanted to lead. I wanted to create jobs; I wanted my brand name at the top of a paycheck, as well as my name being signed to it. Established by me, signed by me.

Again, before ending this chapter, I need you to know: You can be a WORKER or a THINKER. You can also be both, but I request that you try your hardest to use your brain to THINK. And think outside the box.

It will make your life easier. It will make your path simpler.

Chapter Two:
College vs. Self-Education

When I graduated from high school, I never planned on attending college and focusing on learning. I was just getting by so that I could play sports. I also knew that no one in my family had ever finished college; they had attempted, but never finished. I went to the University of Wisconsin-Stevens Point to play wide receiver straight out of high school. Soon, I realized football was not going to be the thing that took my family and me to the next level. There was so much talent and so many opportunities, but not enough time for each guy to shine.

Once I began to fall away from football, I started to focus on school and actually tried to become more aware of where I was and what I wanted to study. I had always been around people and could say the right things at the right times to make them feel better about their days, so first I thought I should major in psychology. Right away, I found that psychology would personally require too much schooling for me, so I switched my major to business. I had never talked about going into business and had no passion for it. I never even realized that I had been a businessman as a kid, but I had no passion. I liked money, and I liked talking to people.

I gained this passion when I met a guy on my football team who became my friend; his name was Mou Vang. Mou was such a hard worker. He told me that he had managed to save thousands of dollars working at McDonald's while playing on the football team full-time, and he had a daughter. I always wondered: why McDonald's? Why work there? Let me give you a hint: Determination. That's why.

Mou always told me that he felt he had to do what he needed to do to make a way for his daughter, no matter what the thing was. After a while, Mou did not have to explain anymore; he was simply dedicated to hard work.

One day, Mou came to practice very happy with different energy and higher spirits.

I asked him, "What's new, brother?"

Mou showed me a picture of his bill from the other night when he took his family out to eat. The receipt read some number around $1,000, and Mou had paid for it all himself. I was a struggling college student, so being the networker, I am, I asked him how he was able to do that for his family. Mou told me he had quit McDonald's and started selling life insurance to families. I asked Mou how I could sign up for this, and he set up a meeting for me with the same guy he started with. On the day I met with this guy, I was just a regular Pierre who was in school, just getting by so that I could acquire a high-paying job.

I met with him, and he talked with me about ownership, business, and most importantly, the Cashflow Quadrant. The Cashflow Quadrant is a chart that shows the types of people there are in this world. **On the left side of the chart, it shows "Employed" and "Self-Employed," which are people who either work a job or own a business that only they work for individually.** For example, a coffee shop in your town owned by a family; they are self-employed. On the right side of the chart, it shows "Business Owners" and "Investors," which are people who own corporations like Starbucks and people who invest equity in businesses like Starbucks.

What I had come to realize from this meeting was that I was living on the left side of that Cashflow Quadrant, which was the poverty side. I also realized that all along, I was a businessman. I had created my own jobs as a kid. I was making so much money as a kid just doing yard work. My mom used to take my money and say she was taking it as a punishment, even if I had not done anything. **I was a businessman all along, and what I had come to realize from this meeting was that college was giving me the watered-down version of business.** If I wanted to really become more knowledgeable in the business market, I would need to self-educate myself by reading and studying those who had done what I was planning to do. I would need to go out and actually try to start something of my own. **Experience rather than years of staring at a board.**

I realized college professors are not realistic because, in college, they teach you as if you'll never have resources in the career world. **College professors teach you not to fail, as if failure does not have a direct**

correlation to your success in life eventually. College professors teach you as if you will never have help in your field of study, when you probably will never have to do anything alone unless you yourself decide to do so. I realized there was a lot of "gray space" after attending this meeting. I had to deal with evaluating what I had been told about college thus far. We all will face this challenge; you will face the wonder. The thought of wondering: has everything I have learned thus far been a lie? Is it actually for my benefit?

Most of us, after asking ourselves this question, will realize: NO! College is not for your benefit but for your control. It always has been and always will be for your control.

What college did for me was show me that if I really wanted to become a master, I would need to study a master who had already done what I would do in my life. College showed me that, yes, it can be beneficial, but only for those who want to be workers, not entrepreneurs. College will instruct you to learn about one specific area of business. **Self-education will allow you to realize that you can place people in a position to work for you while you think.** The solution will always come more easily.

A quote I never let leave me from Robert Kiyosaki states, *"Entrepreneurs do not need to know a lot about a little, but they need to know a little about a lot."*

That statement alone has so much power because in college, they expect one to be a master's student, as if they didn't have you study hundreds of classes that would never even matter to your survival in life. Another thing that resonates with me is a scene from the Steve Jobs movie where his partner, Steve Wozniak, yells at Steve Jobs and says, "WHAT DO YOU DO?! Everyone else has contributed something to this invention.

"WHAT DID YOU DO?" In my head, the clear answer to that question was "THINK OF IT."

Steve Wozniak and all those other employees helped bring the computer to physical life, but it was Steve Jobs who imagined the computer, who had the idea in the first place. Robert Kiyosaki's quote makes even more sense when you hear a question like that asked of a person like Steve Jobs. Steve Jobs was the THINKER, while all the other employees he had were the WORKERS for his thoughts.

Remember my statement from earlier in the book, that meeting with Mou's partner helped me to realize that I could create high-paying jobs for those who did not want to THINK but wanted to WORK. In Steve Jobs' case, that is all he did. Which one will you become? A WORKER or a THINKER? Which box will you be placed in? Or will you be the person placing people in their boxes? The choice remains yours.

Self-education will allow you not only to become more knowledgeable; it will allow you to ask questions to people in positions who have told you otherwise. It opens up for greater dialogue and more specific thought. Self-education gives you the opportunity to study those who have what you want and have been where you are going. First, you must know where you want to go, or people's opinions will navigate your life. Rather than your dreams and end goals being the leader, a college professor can limit your dreams with their statements because, let's be honest, how high up the corporate ladder can a professor climb? Not very high. Self-education gives you the freedom to not have your dreams crushed by a professor who stopped chasing their dreams decades ago.

As I write this book, I am working at a high school. The other day, I asked the assistant principal if he was working the job he actually dreamed of doing.

He made a face and said, "No." He also stated, "I don't think I dream very much."

Yet, this is the guy who leads almost a thousand kids every day. Can you imagine what his advice would be if you went to him with a question about your dream? If he does not dream, how could he ever give you advice on how to chase yours? He cannot. I'll make the statement that no teacher can direct you on how not to quit on yourself or your dreams, because most teachers, if it were not the profession they chose, would have given up on their dream, if they ever had one.

Never, I repeat, never, allow someone who does not inspire you in any way to give you advice on a dream they never had. Never allow people to diminish a spirit or creation they have not even allowed into their own lives. **Self-education is freedom, and it will show you that college is in no way a comparison to truly mastering the gift that God has given to you.** It is not the gift of knowledge that the college professor thinks he or she is giving to you. Five or six years of self-education are examples like Steve Jobs or Steve Harvey, people who never finished college but changed the world.

Have you ever wondered why regular colleges say what they are teaching is just basic knowledge? Have you ever wondered why they make you go through four or five years of basic knowledge just to make you go back and take another three years to become a master?

Ask yourself: Does that make sense? It is not about your growth. It's a system, a continuous vicious cycle. It is all about your money, the money you will owe after college. The same money that most people are still paying back years after they have finished college. The money they said was just to benefit you and get you through school; that money was never yours. It was given to you to keep the government attached to your pockets for an extended period of time. For a lifetime if you allow them. It was to keep CONTROL OVER YOU.

Chapter Three:
Loyalty Rose

I have always been one of the most loyal people in a group. I have always had long-lasting friendships and bonds with my past friends. I have always been able to be loyal no matter how others were acting. I realized early on that loyalty was a huge part of my personality, and in sixth grade, I wrote a name. I wrote "LOYALTY ROSE MCCOY."

I never knew I would have a child, let alone a daughter, but I always had this name ready just in case. I always thought of having a baby girl simply because I knew how to be a man. It was hard to understand women for some reason, and at a very young age, I believed a daughter would help me do so much better. I had written that name when I was a kid, and I never forgot it. I knew I would like to name my offspring Loyalty Rose.

Loyalty is what I base my core values upon, outside of love, and the rose is my favorite flower. No flower is as beautiful as a rose, and the word "loyalty" is one of the most powerful words there is. The name always had meaning to me. I just never knew it would become the most meaningful thing in my life one day.

The wild thing is, I wrote in my high school yearbook this exact statement, "I want to have one baby girl, spoil her, & have her with me all the time."

Literally, that is exactly how my path transpired.

While I was attending Stevens Point, I was dating a girl back home in my city. I had stopped playing football, and I just had way too much free time at school before I started to take my time seriously. I would regularly go home on the weekends, which was like a two-hour drive, just to see my girlfriend. Doing that ultimately caught up to me. I was falling for her; I was always a "lover boy." I loved for the prettiest girl to always be called mine, and trust me, she always was.

I was at Stevens Point, and she was all the way in Atlanta for college. We were just trying to make it work. She came home because she was having tuition problems at school, and it was a situation she had to handle right away. While she was home, that is when I started going home every weekend to visit her. One night at school, I got a call from my girl back home saying that she thought she was pregnant. I did not believe her at first because I ultimately never had sexual interactions with any woman unless I was using protection. This night, though, I remember loosening my boundaries to raise her satisfaction. So, it was possible that she was not lying. I hitched a ride home from school as soon as possible so that I could be home when she went to the hospital to see if she was pregnant or not.

To my disbelief, she was pregnant, and I had created a new challenge in my life that I was in no position to handle. She was also in the midst of figuring out her school situation. I dropped everything at Stevens Point and transferred back home to Milwaukee to attend Wisconsin Lutheran College, and she never went back to Atlanta. In this phase of my life, I struggled immensely; I still struggle. I didn't know how to be a dad, and I was a broke college student. For a while, I asked why, I complained, and I just was not ready. I evaluated myself and realized that I was thinking all wrong. I was thinking of MYSELF when it was no longer time to do that.

My daughter, Loyalty, had become my "why." She had become my deciding factor on every choice I made. Once I changed my mindset, nothing I did started with me thinking of myself. All my decisions began with my daughter, Loyalty in mind. **I truly believe God does that purposely to people He truly sees greatness in. God will send you something or make something happen in your life that completely alters your decision-making for the better.** Loyalty completely and undoubtedly changed my perception of life and the decisions I was finalizing before she entered my world.

Everything became more of a weight, but I was becoming a better person all around. College got harder. How did I finish? If I didn't, how could I ever tell Loyalty to finish? Football practice got longer, and I was on the bus. How did I finish the season? I told the coach I had a daughter, and the whole team knew, so I got leeway to come a bit later to practice. If I lied to my coaches and made excuses as to why I could not make it to every practice, what advice would I have to give my daughter if she happens to go through the same situation in her life? Loyalty brought the gift of truth into my life. I started to tell the truth, and I started to be set free.

One thing I believe is true about life is that everyone has a story that God has written about them. If you are a truth-teller, you have a great chance of accomplishing what God has set out for you to accomplish. If you are a liar, you are throwing the TRUE LIFE off balance because you are deciding with your free will to make a lie out of the story of truth that God has written for you. You are altering the path. **Life will challenge you daily with lies just to see if you will ever return to the truth. There can only be one true you, and God has already decided on who that should be.**

Not only did Loyalty make me become truthful, but she also made me decide to become a true entrepreneur. I knew I never wanted her to work a job unless it was for a company that I owned.

While at Wisconsin Lutheran College, I finished reading my first book ever, called *Before You Quit Your Job* by Robert Kiyosaki. The book changed my world even more. It gave me a clearer visual of what Mou's mentor meant in our meeting. I also got a taste of what that hard work meant for Mou, always having to provide for his daughter. Robert Kiyosaki, in his book, explained his story and his struggles with the Cashflow Quadrant precisely, and how he became the multi-millionaire entrepreneur he is today.

The most important message from that book for me is the statement, "You can become your own paycheck." Can you imagine a check with not only your name on it, but written by your corporation or brand? You should be living on your assets. You should be driving in your asset. Anything you associate yourself with and that you value, you should own.

Loyalty placed a fire under my butt; I want and strive to give her a life I always imagined or greater. Why not? Why should your child live the life you lived? Why should your child have to feel the pain you caused? I had to realize this, and I have faith that whoever is reading this does, too, one day.

God sent Loyalty to give me a second chance at life. An update on my view of life. She is a replica of me, meant to do better, to become what I've always wanted to become, in order for her to have a successful future. Never forget that your child is God's child, and He can send you a gift as well as take your gift away. Parents lose children every day for multiple reasons. The main reason is a lack of care for their child. If you are choosing not to care about your child, you are showing God again that you will do nothing with your second chance.

Always remember: God does all things for the greater good and to benefit His children. God knew Loyalty would light a fire under my butt. God knew Loyalty would push me in ways I may have never pushed myself if He had never sent her as a gift. Loyalty helped me find Robert Kiyosaki. Loyalty motivated me to start developing my mind and becoming wiser. Loyalty is the reason I graduated from school. Loyalty is the reason I read my first book, *Before You Quit Your Job*. Loyalty is the reason I am writing my first book as well. If you allow it, your children are sent not only to change you, but to change your life.

Chapter Four:
Before You Quit Your Job

I was really determined after the meeting with Mou's counterpart. I was calling everybody back home, telling them college was wasting my time and that I should be at home creating. I wanted to quit school so many times after returning home from Stevens Point, especially after having my daughter Loyalty. I was now in school at Wisconsin Lutheran College with a daughter and a hope to start a business.

Before attending Wisconsin Lutheran College, I had never finished a book in my entire life on my own. I was always assisted in completing my book reports or assignments that dealt with reading books. That was until I was introduced to Robert Kiyosaki, the famous author of the *Rich Dad Poor Dad* series. I had found out about him after meeting Mou's partner. I started to watch all types of motivational speakers, from Eric Thomas to Tony Robbins.

I was so intrigued after hearing what Mou's partner had to say that I started to self-educate. I started to watch a lot of motivational videos, and one day, I came across Robert Kiyosaki on YouTube. He made the statement that the rich and wealthy had told him not to give away the information he was giving away on YouTube. He stated they wanted to keep the poor poorer and the rich richer. "Keep them poor," he had said. I watched this video and just started to study him on YouTube.

I had never taken an interest in any of his books until one day I was in the library renting movies, and I happened to walk by the books. I saw his book, *Before You Quit Your Job*. I decided to rent the book out and challenge myself to finish it. During the time I was reading the book, I was working at Starbucks and Abercrombie & Fitch. For some reason, even though I made money, I have always disliked working a job. For a long time, I had never finished an entire year at a job. I was always going back to finding another way to try to bring in some money, so when I saw this book, I thought I had to read it. I felt it was crucial for me to read it, to prove to myself and to show my commitment.

I started to read this book, and I began hanging notes on my closet door in my apartment. I had always been a note-taker, but never like this. I did not want to miss anything important that Robert Kiyosaki was saying in the book, so I would always pause and write it down. Every time I finished a chapter, I added more notes to my closet door. I felt as if I was gaining so much knowledge just based on his explaining the difference between his rich dad's mindset and his poor dad's mindset. The mindsets were at times similar, but the stamina behind the plan each father had in mind is what, in the end, made the distinguishing differences in the two fathers' lives.

"How bad do you want it?"

This is a question you must ask yourself if you are truly going to change not only your life, but your family's life. Are you willing to give everything you have, even your life, to obtain the dream and master the gift God has sent you to this earth to nurture? In his book, Robert Kiyosaki shares many moments when he could have quit, but his persistence and stamina kept him going because of his passion for his dream, and the knowledge his rich dad was able to give him. He never quit. Will you quit?

Robert did not quit because he had two mentors giving him two different types of advice. I believe Robert Kiyosaki never quit because he watched his actual dad start and quit on his dreams. At the same time, he had a dad who quit on himself and his dreams. Robert's friend's dad was rich and could give Robert the visual he needed and wanted. Robert did not quit because he made a choice between the two visuals he was getting: a poor visual and a rich visual. Although both these people were people Robert cared about, he knew which life he wanted to live, and he chose it.

A key quote I've always held onto from Jesse Itzler, a well-known entrepreneur, is, *"The more you experience, the more you have to offer."*

Kiyosaki had the perspective of a life guided by a rich man and a poor man, and these experiences ultimately gave him a story he could not only share with the world but also use to teach and inspire others. Now, it's your turn. What will you choose? What is your stamina like behind your dream? What have you experienced? How many doors will you allow to be shut in your face before you quit? Doors will be slammed; people are not going to believe in you, that is inevitable. The greatest question every human must ask themselves is: Do you believe in yourself? Do you believe that you can do it? If God has for certain written you a story of prosperous success, the greatest question you must ask yourself is: Do you believe in yourself?

As I continued to read his book and got closer to the end, I realized I wanted to quit both my jobs and try to cut grass full-time. I had come to this realization, but I was not sure; I was not confident. However, I gained my confidence when I read a chapter in the book where Robert spoke about how your first business is your PRACTICE BUSINESS. If you fail, everything you learned from that first business, its successes and failures, you will be able to apply to help you start a new business and run it even better than you thought you could before.

Kiyosaki stated that first, you had to come up with an idea. I would have to create something or sell something. What should I create? Could I create something? Yes, OF COURSE! Can YOU? Yes, OF COURSE you can; but first you must believe. You must believe that you can. You must have faith in not only your idea, but in yourself being capable of making that idea come to life. The right person will abide by your rules and follow your journey with you in faith of your dream coming true.

Never lower your WISHES. Never lower your EXPECTATIONS. Never lower your IMAGINATION. Never lower your PRICES. Believe in what you are bringing to the table and always bet on YOU. Believe in the value of you. Believe in your vision. Believe in the value of your creation.

One important note to end this chapter: Robert Kiyosaki often emphasizes taking bold action and owning your ideas in the business world. While he doesn't say these exact words, the principle is clear: when creating a product or service, you can choose to position yourself at the highest price, the lowest, or the middle, but true impact comes from being bold and unique. **Nobody has your idea but you. Go bring it to life, for yourself and the world to see.**

Chapter Five:
QuickFastQuality

Every summer for a long time, while I was in high school and college, I would use my mom's lawnmower to walk around the neighborhood and cut people's grass for extra money. I knew a ton of people because of how often I would do it, but I was never "legit." I only cut their grass; I did not have a leaf blower or an edge trimmer. I only had a lawnmower, and the clients did not even have my contact info.

After finishing Robert Kiyosaki's book, *Before You Quit Your Job*, I decided I was going to start a landscaping business. I did a test: I created the name I would call my landscaping company.

The name of it is **"QuickFastQuality: Seasonal Yard Care Services."** I know it's a long name, but it was mine, and I created it in MY MIND. I ordered business cards and went to my mom's neighborhood. I started walking to each of my clients' doors, giving out my business cards and letting them know I planned on going legit. All of them were saying positive things like, "These cards look nice," "I'll be calling you," and "When are you available?"

All positive remarks. I knew I was going to do it; I was sure I was going to do it. But then I thought: Who am I going to do it with? I did not have transportation or a lawnmower. The summer I decided to start my business with my mom's lawnmower, it was stolen. I had to think quickly, so I did.

My "brother from another mother," Evan Wilder, was my best friend in high school, and at the time I decided to create the business, he was not doing much. I talked with him about my idea, and for a while, he was not into it. That was until I told him the statement that had stuck with me from Robert Kiyosaki's book, which went like this: "We can be our own paycheck."

I kept telling Evan things from the book and how I had a plan and how we could do it. He finally said yes.

After getting Evan to confirm, I knew I had transportation and strength. Now I needed one more body. As a kid, as I spoke about in earlier chapters, I had always created a job for myself because of how well I networked with people. Not only did I create jobs for myself, but I also created jobs for my older cousin, Corvon Stephens. My cousin and I were very close as kids. Our moms always seemed to move either next to each other if possible or down the block from one another; they always wanted to be close. I would always bring my cousin with me to go make money, whether it was shoveling snow, cutting grass, or raking leaves. We had already done it all together as kids. I knew he would be interested in the opportunity. I ran it by him and let him know Evan was already in. Of course, I was not surprised when he said yes.

I now had my team. Now it was time to acquire equipment and get to work. We were all still working at jobs at the time, so I let them know that with our next checks, we would put some money together and grab a new lawnmower. We all worked, and in a few weeks, we all chipped in, and Evan and I went to Menards and picked up a lawnmower. Our journey had begun. I started an Instagram page for the business, and we got started. Right away, friends and family started to book us for weekly and bi-weekly services, and we were even doing a lot for the principal of a middle school.

We started off doing well, but I was still working at Starbucks. I started to miss work at Starbucks because I did not want to put Starbucks before work that I had created on my own. After a few days of call-ins and one day of being late by an hour because I had cut two lawns before coming into work, Starbucks decided to let me go. Starbucks did not let me go in a regular fashion. I met with both the store manager and the district manager, and they both complimented me on how great a worker I was, but said they could not have me putting my business over my Starbucks job. I was fired, but I was enlightened. I was great to them, and the reason I was being let go, in my eyes, was inspiring.

I left to begin my own journey. My journey to own something I thought up in my own head with my own brainwaves. Have you ever wondered what you could be creating or who you could be hiring if you just decided to say no to working for others and yes to more thinking and creating for others? After I was fired, I went full-fledged with **QuickFastQuality**.

I asked Evan and Corvon if they could stop working their jobs so they could see if we could start to make some serious money. It took both of them a while, but they did. For the first few months, we were making money, nice money, weekly, daily, whenever we wanted to go out, but we still did not have all the proper equipment. We were getting a quality job done, but it was a hassle because while our lawnmower was new, our edge trimmer was old, and the leaf blower was electric and had to be plugged in. Everything was inconvenient.

Until one day, after a long day of cutting grass, I decided to stop at an old neighbor's home that I knew when I used to live in my old neighborhood. The names of the people whose house it was were Shar Borg and Peter Borg. Shar is one of the most generous, kindhearted women you will ever meet in life. She is also the leading real estate agent in Wisconsin history, selling millions of dollars in real estate a year. I decided to stop at her house just to give her a business card. She was sitting in her backyard on her laptop handling business, and I walked up and said, "Hey, Shar."

She was so excited to see me, gave me a hug, and asked me what I was doing. I gave her my card and let her know I had started a landscaping business. She was so amazed and started to ask me questions about how I got the idea and how it was going. I remember her saying, "You built a team that fast? It took me years to build a team."

After meeting with her, I felt not only super excited to keep pushing my business, but like I had sensed a tiny bit of interest. Interest in my business meant she might invest in my startup. I had this chip on my shoulder and this thought that would not leave my mind; I kept thinking, "What if she wants to invest?"

Finally, I asked Evan's dad, who was one of my employees at the time, what he thought. I told him about mine and Shar's entire conversation. Evan's dad thought it would be in my best interest to see if my thought was correct. I still did not feel sure, so I called another one of my mentors, who was my middle school teacher from sixth grade, with whom I was still close, Chelsea Prochnow. She said something similar, that I should reach out to her and see if my thought was correct.

Ultimately, I got the confidence to send her a text message and ask her if she would invest in my business. She did not respond the first day, but when she did, she let me know she would definitely be interested in investing; but first, I would have to meet with her and her husband. I ended up meeting with them, and I brought one of my employees, Evan, with me because I thought they were just going to cut me a check.

Although I had written out at least a nine-and-a-half-page business plan, which included my mission statement, research on all the competition in the area, and research on how much the landscaping market was worth in 2018, I really thought I was prepared, but I was not. Shar and her husband asked me questions I was not prepared for, like, "What if we give you this money and you want to buy your daughter a nice gift?"

I was so surprised; I felt offended. I was thinking, "Why bring me here to ask me this? If you do not trust me, do not invest." I realized as time went on that those were amazing questions, and if they were not going to ask me, who would?

The questions they were asking made me uncomfortable because they were not about my business or my plan. I soon realized they did not care much about my plan, but about their money. Shar wanted me to start getting better with money, and after that meeting, I was very agitated, but I never got angry again. I became even more passionate. I wanted them to trust me right away, but I had not earned it. I didn't deserve it. **I had to earn it, step by step.**

I remember when I was setting up my LLC because Shar insisted that I do so. While I was setting it up, the bank offered me a business credit card, and I was so scared. I did not know whether to say yes or no; I put the bank on pause, and I called Shar. She answered, and I told her why I called.

She stated, "Pierre, never be afraid of money; God put money here as a tool for you and me."

She told me never to worship money, because that is when a problem arises. I hung up the phone with her and said, "Yes," to the credit card. I realized that Shar believed in ME! Shar saw something in me that she had seen in herself, and that is why she invested in me.

Over the next few weeks, Shar had me go through a number of tests, and we would meet on Fridays. The first Friday, she had me bring her around $350–$400 in cash because I told her I could make that easily in a week, so that is what I did. The second Friday, she told me she wouldn't invest unless I had an LLC business bank account set up first. If you're wondering what an LLC is, it stands for Limited Liability Company. This means that if anyone ever sues me, they can only go after my business assets, not my personal ones. I did not enjoy this part because I had a problem finding a bank I could trust. I had to wait longer than I wanted to for the investment; this made me mentally patient. I was so impatient before. I wanted everything right away, always chasing instant gratification.

During those few weeks before Shar actually invested in the company, I learned that instant gratification was nothing but a shortcut. A shortcut would mean giving in to my impulses, to my desires, and I realized I needed to control myself, to move with discipline. A shortcut would either make my business fail or put me in a position where I would need to recover. I never wanted to deal with that either.

So, I finally got my business LLC, and I felt accomplished. I had not even gotten the check yet, but the simple investment in something I owned felt so good. Finally, Evan and I visited Shar on the third Friday, and she was very busy. I showed her the confirmation from my LLC and the information she wanted. She smiled and sent me the money, and I put it in my business bank account. She told me she was not only proud but excited for me. So was I. I was so proud and excited. I was proud of myself, of this company, and happy that I had gone with this idea, the one God had placed in me and implanted in my heart.

On this day, I was able to realize that the things I thought about came to life. **If it was MEANT to happen and I thought about it, it would come to life. I want all of you who are reading this book to know: I started my landscaping business from a THOUGHT.** I had always been a businessman; I had always loved working for myself, but I never knew it all this time. All I had to do was "think" my dreams into action.

The book, *Before You Quit Your Job,* by Robert Kiyosaki, woke me up from my sleeping dreams. It allowed me to remember my childhood and to realize I already had a business; I just needed a strategy and a brand. **Reading that book allowed me to realize I was not meant only to be a worker, but a THINKER as well.** I was meant to thread the needle; I was meant to be the first.

What are you meant to be? Whose life are you meant to change? What will you create? Or will you never ever make an attempt? The choice remains yours.

Chapter Six:
Challenges

My first year in business owning QuickFastQuality was a rush. When I say rush, I mean like you're late to your favorite musician's concert, you aren't ready yet, and you know you're gonna run into traffic! Everything happened so fast. Everything was going so well; we were making money consistently and had a growing, stable client base. Evan was letting us use his car to get to the clients, so we had transportation. I also had the recent investment and the business credit card. Shar Borg, my investor, was even sending us to cut the lawns of the homes she was selling before she sold them.

Everything was going great. I was controlling everything myself: the equipment, the payroll, the client communication, the bookkeeping, and the social media marketing and posts. I was doing it all. The biggest problem was the fact that it took me too long to realize I could not handle it all. I tried to get Evan and Corvon to start doing their own bookkeeping, asking them to start writing down what I was paying them for their own records. I wanted them to start taking on some responsibility.

Evan always let us use his car, but his energy started to waver. I could see that he started to dislike that we were always putting wear and tear on his vehicle. Evan and Corvon worked for me, but they had their own dreams. Although they worked for me, I could always see that I loved the business, but they did not love it as much as I did. **It was my creation; it wasn't theirs. No matter how much I wanted to make it feel like theirs, too, it wasn't.** I always felt I went a little harder than both of them did, and when I tried to go hard on them, I do not believe they liked it because they did not care as much as I did.

I realized too late that I needed a bigger team. I was not controlling the money correctly; I was not making wise decisions with the profits. I was everywhere. I was mixing my personal life with my business, and honestly, for a while, I made the two accounts one and the same. **I was**

overwhelmed, and things began to change for me. I was still finishing college at WLC while having this business and clients who still needed me. Because I was controlling everything,

Corvon and Evan could not handle any clients without me, so things started to get jammed-packed. I had clients calling me while I was in class, asking if I was available. I had scheduled clients I was going to see before class, and I was late to class.

I was juggling a lot and still trying not to let my creation fail. I was leaving classes early; I let my professors know I had a business and made them aware of my situation. Some were okay with it; most were not. I was still able to get my work done and obtain passing grades, but was I really focusing on school? No. Ultimately, I made it through the first year at Wisconsin Lutheran College without losing my business.

I had even acquired two contracts at the beginning of the summer that were huge. One was a school called St. Marcus Lutheran School, the same school I was expelled from in fourth grade. God brought me back to the same place where I was not the best person when I was younger, to shine light on my older, greater self. I also acquired a contract with a Mobil gas station. It was an amazing start to the summer, or so I thought.

One night, I, Evan, and our other brother, Jakob, were longboarding downtown. We were just rolling through downtown Milwaukee like we always did, just cruising. I remember this hill that Jakob and I had always wanted to go down; we were literally going the totally opposite way, but we decided to turn around. We went to the hill and went all the way to the top. Before going down, we all had a weird energy about the steep hill, and we did not know just how steep it was or how fast we would be going.

We all started down the hill on our boards, and we were flying! I mean, we were going at least 25–30 mph on our longboards. At that speed, it is very hard to slow down, and Evan and Jakob are both heavy-set guys. We were all just going down the hill yelling because we were going so fast. I heard Evan yelling, and I heard Jakob yelling, so I thought we were all good. Three or four meters before the end of the hill, there were people walking on the path. Jakob dodged them, I dodged them, but Evan fell before he could dodge them. We heard Evan yelling, but he usually falls and jokes, so we made nothing of it.

The two people who were walking yelled, "I think your friend is really hurt!"

Jakob and I ran down the hill, and to our surprise, Evan had broken his ankle in a horrible way. I had to run like 12 blocks to his house to grab the car because we were on longboards. I led his dad to him and Jakob, and we went to the hospital. Evan had broken his ankle, and he was one of my employees. I had to start the summer with my cousin Corvon as my only worker. Evan was the second-best employee after me, and Corvon was the third, but he was working his way up. I really wish that had never happened to Evan because it affected the business in a big way.

I started having trouble getting in touch with Corvon. He was not coming to work; he just stopped wanting to help. This was undoubtedly the most clients I had ever had in the summer, and I was alone. I was cutting two whole school campuses alone, and I was also still cutting my regular clients. Thankfully, Evan was still allowing me to use his car to get to the clients. I was putting a lot of strain on my body and mind. I was too tired to hang out with my daughter and her mom. I never had time to do anything besides cut grass. I was one-dimensional. I made money, but every other aspect of my life was going downhill. I was becoming overwhelmed, but I never quit.

My work was affecting my love life and the relationship with my daughter's mother. Unfortunately, at the end of my second summer owning my business, all my equipment started breaking down. Both my lawn mowers went out, as did my edger trimmer; I even lost my ax.

Everything was going badly. I had to start telling clients my equipment was down. I was losing money and client loyalty. I didn't know when I would be able to acquire equipment again because I was managing money poorly.

Ultimately, when I started school back up, QuickFastQuality was on pause. I was basically in recovery mode. I could not get anything to go right. I started school back up, but I would still try to get landscaping jobs on the weekends, and Evan would let me use his car. One weekend, Evan let me use his car for leaf-blowing clients. He told me I could keep it overnight. I had to finish my clients, and I also needed to wash my clothes. I asked Evan's parents if I could come by to wash my clothes there because my washer and dryer at home were not good ones; they let me. I brought my daughter's mom with me, washed my clothes, said bye to Evan's parents, and headed home.

As we were driving home, I was super tired. It had been a long day of driving and working. I felt myself keep dozing off, so I let my window down a bit. I got off the freeway and made a right turn. I remember driving up the hill a block or two away from my house. Next thing I knew, my daughter's mom was screaming, "Oh my God! PIERRE! PIERRE!" I opened my eyes, and I was on the curb, about to drive into someone's house. I hit the brakes, drove off the curb, and went home. Evan's entire front bumper and both front tires were shattered with bent rims. I had almost fallen asleep behind the wheel of a car that was not even mine. I called Evan and let him know; he was not happy. I believe that, to this day, this is one of the things that put a strain on our brotherhood.

It was very intriguing to me how fast things started to change in my life. **I started to lose friends, and I lost the relationship with my daughter's mother. My business was on pause. Most of all, I was starting to lose myself.** I was trying to force all these things and people to stay in my life when God did not want them there. **I was trying to force all these people to have a dream they did not want. If you can learn anything from this chapter, it is that when God wants something to happen in your life, He does not have to ask your permission.**

You will go through challenges in life, and you will question yourself and God because you believe you have your own best interest at heart when you do not. God does not want to control your life; He wants you to control it. **God wants you to choose Him to lead your life and your decisions. Only you can control what you decide; that is called free will.** God wants to be chosen to lead. Only then can you not only understand your challenges, but also overcome them.

One of the biggest challenges I have ever had was letting go of my daughter's mom. I wanted my daughter to have a family so badly. I did not come from a married household, and my daughter's mom did not either. **I wanted to break the curse; I strongly believed I would. God did not have that written for me, though, and I went against it for so long. It did nothing but get me in trouble.** It did nothing but put who I actually was on the back burner to become whom she wanted me to be. I went on trips I knew I could not afford because I wanted to make her happy. I did so many things to try to make her stay, but ultimately God showed me, "Pierre, she is not for you."

He showed me in the worst way. He literally had to hurt me so many times, and I still wouldn't let go. She had even told me she did not love me and to leave her alone after years. I did not believe her; I still pursued. I always pursued this toxic love because I wanted my daughter to be brought up in a different way. God did not see it as such, but I would not let go until God forced me to. One day, Janiya and I got into an argument; she put me in a sleeper hold, and I bit her thumb. After doing this, Janiya called the cops on me even though I was only defending myself. I, unfortunately, was taken to jail for two days.

I never felt the same about Janiya again. Not only did she tell the cops she did not want me arrested, but she also only wanted it on my record. I allowed her to make me make a decision that would jeopardize my ability to see my daughter; she wanted this. She wanted to see me down. She wanted me to know she did not feel the way I felt. I never listened, so God made me listen. **I have a firm belief in life: God will do things the easy way or the hard way. The choice remains yours.**

God gave me so many outs; He gave me so many clues I never took because I was leaning on my own understanding. Never do that. Never believe you have your best interest at heart without acknowledging God first. **I want you to know that challenges will come up in your life, but you can overcome them and defeat them way faster than it took me. Allow my story and my message to sit with you; compare them to your life.**

Do you have challenges you are facing that God is trying to lead you through? Are you ignoring God in any way, like I was? Are you forcing something or someone to be in your life? Answer all these questions for yourself. Allow yourself to grow; first, you must know where God is challenging you to grow. Allow life's challenges, whether you fail or succeed, to propel you forward.

Chapter Seven:
Failure Will Propel You

As I spoke about in earlier chapters, I failed sixth grade. I failed, but that failure propelled me. If I had never failed, I can say for sure that I would have been on a continuous path of expulsion from different middle schools. If I had never failed sixth grade, I would have never met Ms. Heinen and Ms. Procknow, two teachers who helped me make it all the way through to graduation. Ms. Procknow and Ms. Heinen are still available today when I need guidance. **God had it planned for me to fail sixth grade so that it would propel me to my future.**

I wanted to attend Wisconsin Lutheran College when I graduated from high school, but I didn't have the GPA required to get in. I applied twice and even wrote a letter explaining why I would be a good fit, but I still did not get in. God worked His wonders when I had Loyalty. I was attending the University of Wisconsin-Stevens Point, but I didn't want to commute two hours back and forth to see my daughter, so I transferred to Wisconsin Lutheran College. I got in right away. Life will show you, if you pay attention, that God does give you what you want. Never when you want it, though, but when you need it. God did not see me starting school at Wisconsin Lutheran College because I wanted it, but when I needed to be home, He gave me what I wanted all along. The failure I had getting into Wisconsin Lutheran College the first time would only propel me to get in later in life.

My sophomore year in high school, I attended the semifinals for the high jump. If I placed high enough, I could go to the state. It had been a while since a high jumper from our school had gone to the state. I came to the meeting so unprepared and so out of it. I didn't even jump 5'10", and that was an easy height for me. As a sophomore, I did not care at the time until I saw the disappointment and anger on my coach's face. He had driven hours out of his way in excitement that I would make it far, and I had not even given my best; I was not even prepared.

After that season, I never gave that level of effort again. I always gave my best, and it started to pay off. In my senior year, not only did I make it to state for the high jump, but my teammate and I both made it and both placed at state. David got second, and I got a third-place medal. I jumped out of my shoes that day; I jumped 6'5", and I was only 6'2". My energy and adrenaline that day were amazing. If I had never failed my sophomore year and seen my coach's face of defeat, I would have never gone on to state my senior year and placed. I would have had no reason to show the change I had made if I had never failed.

If I had never failed, God would not have given me the opportunity to be the push that helped my teammate become better, too. **God uses you and your failure not always only to benefit you, but to benefit others. The failures you and I go through in life shape us; they mold us into the people we are going to be.** If you are destined to change your family's path and you never go through the struggle it takes to get there, how will you ever accomplish what is meant for you?

Failure is directly correlated with success when dealt with correctly. **When I say failure has a direct correlation with success, I mean you can fail 50 times trying to get your driver's license, but the one time you finally pass, you have succeeded.** It is not like every time you fail, you get farther and farther away from your license; that is not the way the world works. It only works that way if you have a negative outlook on your failure. Only success matters in the long run. No one but you will care about all the failures you had to deal with to become successful, but you will.

You will realize, as life goes on, that *that* is all that matters.

The same thing goes for your dreams, sports, and life period. **The more you do things over and over and over again, if you are positive about your failure, every time you do it over, if you truly pay attention, you learn.** The one time you finally get it right, it is like all those times you failed never even mattered, but they did. The fact that you chose to have a positive outlook on your failure allowed you to react better to success emotionally. It is how you deal with failure that will determine the direction your life goes in. **I have failed and continue to fail as I go on through my journey in life. It is a challenge for everyone, but anyone who expects the challenge will exceed the expectations placed on their life. Faith that your failure has a purpose will always propel you.**

God states in Jeremiah 29:11 that He has plans to prosper you, plans to give you hope and a future. **The only way to ruin God's plan is to not have faith in it. God also shows you, through your failure, that it was always part of the plan; He will give you a glimpse of sunlight you never expected or thought possible, allowing you to see the plan revealed and that the failure was not for nothing.** In order for this glimpse of light to be revealed to you, you have to have a positive outlook on your failure. If you are negatively going about things and reacting to your failure, you are showing God that you not only don't believe in Him, but that you don't believe He cares enough about you to make your failure worthwhile.

Only those who learn nothing from failure are the true losers. Because if you outlast the pain, the naysayers, the "no's," and the slammed doors, if you outlast all the family members, friends, and significant others telling you to quit, you will realize all that you went through was only molding you and strengthening you so that you would be prepared for the bright future that God has written for you.

If God gives you something you do not believe in, it will not only overwhelm you but also make you fear it because you are unaware of its capabilities or how it will affect your life. That is why He prepares us by giving us trials and tribulations. Preparation is the sole purpose of human challenges.

I never thought I would get a second chance at Wisconsin Lutheran College. I never thought they would ever consider me after denying me so many times. I struggled at Wisconsin Lutheran College, but what I did know was that I struggled at Stevens Point as well. I knew if I could struggle at one place and get so close to succeeding, I could do the same at Wisconsin Lutheran College. God had prepared me. I had just transferred from Stevens Point, which had an entirely new curriculum. I had also lost a lot of credits from my other university because they were two different types of schools, so I technically had to do two extra years of schooling.

I was so ready to be done with school, and I did not think I would make it at Wisconsin Lutheran College. I always kept faith, though, that I could not quit school. I never once, out of my entire five-year tenure at college, wanted to QUIT. I had doubts and regrets, but I never wanted to quit because I had put too much time into it. After two years of struggle, tears, and bus rides, I became a first-generation graduate. I graduated from Wisconsin Lutheran College with a bachelor's degree in business administration. No one else in my family has yet finished a four-year degree.

God put me through all that failure at a young age, failing sixth grade, being in all that trouble as an elementary kid, and constantly getting beatings from my mom and dad, and being told I was the bad kid. **I turned out to be the "chosen one."**

All of my challenges, expulsions, and failures were preparation to PROPEL ME FORWARD. I was the first in my family to break two curses: I started my own business in college with a newborn daughter, and I graduated with a four-year degree while raising a two-year-old and holding on to a struggling relationship. God works in mysterious ways; no failure or fault you have will not have a reason. How will you be the first in your family? What curses will you break? What failure in your life thus far could you acknowledge has PROPELLED YOU?

Chapter Eight:
Never Be a Follower

I have never been a follower, and I've always been disliked because of it. I would never follow all the guys to chase after a girl; I'd get the girl's number and talk to her on my own time. I would never follow friends to parties or into trouble. I was the leader; people followed me into trouble, although I never got into much trouble. I was the guy whom all the guys talked about at the lunch table because I had the girl every guy wanted, or I was going after the girl the strongest guy had. I made myself noticeable because while you would see everyone else in the crowd, you would see me hanging by myself. I have always chosen to be the outlier, and in my experience, it has benefited my life.

It has benefited me, and it can benefit you as well. **In order to get what you want out of life, you must be willing at some point to not be liked. It is easy to follow the crowd because everyone is doing the same thing.** If someone in the crowd sees you trying to step outside of the box, they will either make fun of you or make you feel unwanted. All this is envy. The person watching you leave the crowd wishes they had the strength to do what they truly want, but they don't.

In life, from my experience, if you wait too long to choose YOURSELF and your PURPOSE over the crowd, you will never achieve success or fulfill your purpose. In that case, you are worthless without a purpose for your life. If you choose to follow in someone else's footsteps and you fail, is it their fault? No. Only you should lead your life. What you allow inside of your mind and heart will ultimately direct your life.

I always tell people: if you have not tried something, do not speak on it. My feelings, values, and emotions are all mine. I might not like a movie for personal reasons; if I tell you not to watch it because I don't like it, and you don't, you just missed out on an experience that might have been fun for you because of my personal feelings. **Always allow yourself to feel. Allow yourself to think and feel before making a**

choice that could affect you in the long run.

Life is like chess; you have to think critically before you make any move because one wrong move and you could lose a powerful counterpart or lose the game altogether. **Never allow people to feel for you, because they may express what you feel in the wrong way, and you will be held accountable for it.** Again, similar to chess, never let someone choose your move for you; it's your game.

Let's switch out the word "game" with "life." If you knew you could lose the game, meaning your life, and you die if you lose, would you allow another human who is not you to make a decision on the direction your game is going? A huge problem in society today is the internet. You may have just gone through a breakup or been fired from a job. You may not know how to express your emotions, so you go online and find a MEME that seems to say what you feel. You post it and send it to friends in hopes that the world will understand how you feel or what kind of person you are. It does not have that effect. Those words in that MEME are not your feelings; that is how someone else feels. **They just know how to express themselves, and you don't; I call that being a follower. You are following someone else's emotions.**

Yes, they may have gone through a similar situation or even the same situation. **But how that person expresses their emotions does not make them your emotions. All you are doing is relating to them; you aren't actually expressing how YOU feel.** You are sympathizing with how they are feeling, and that's okay. But if you cannot express YOUR feelings, YOUR emotions, and YOUR views in a situation, you are not being yourself; you are being a follower. If you are interested in certain things but you know the people you hang around think it's weird, so you don't do it, not only are you a follower, you are altering a path that could potentially be meant for you.

Lead your own life. Do not be afraid to go your own way and not be liked for a while in order to make your dreams come true. Success does not happen by accident; it is intentional. It is planned, committed to, and grasped. Success is available to everyone, but not everyone has the ability or the will to choose themselves. Everyone wants a thousand followers or a thousand friends, but most of those people do not have a thousand dollars. Which one would you rather have? A thousand friends who are holding you back from your purpose, or a thousand dollars you could use to benefit yourself and others?

Again, I have never been the most likable person because I have never been a follower. No one likes the loner; no one likes the person who chooses to put in hours alone to make their dreams come true rather than wasting time with friends at parties. **We all have two due dates in life: the due date of our birth and the due date of our death. Knowing that we did not get to control either of those dates, wouldn't you like to control your life while you are living?**

In life, people like to live their entire lives living for other people, allowing others to think and decide for them. Once those decisions are set in stone, whatever image was portrayed as you, only you will deal with the consequences, even if you did not think or decide. Once you give away your responsibility to decide, you give away your image.

Never forget that you will be remembered through life and death. In life, people decide on who you are to them, and those same people, whether you are dead or alive, will give that same portrayal to others. The legacy you leave on this earth matters because all of you reading this book will produce offspring. The children you have will have to live their own lives as well, and the history and legacy you leave will never leave you or them. The offspring you produce will have to live under the umbrella of your legacy. No matter what they do, who their parents were, or what they did, it will matter to their future.

Who will remember you, though? Do you ever ask yourself that question? If all your life you have been following other people and never took the time to try your own path or build your own table, who will you be remembered as? The person who accomplishes their dreams and helps benefit the world through creation and innovation, or the person who was complacent and did the same thing every day, drinking and smoking their life away? The choice is yours, which person you will become. I can assure you that the two types of lives each choice entails are totally different. You get one life, only one; don't waste it being a follower of people who have no destination.

Life is about challenges, ups, and downs. If you are always following in someone else's footsteps, you will not endure the challenges you need to go through in order to master YOU. It is very possible to be so consumed with following someone else that their problems start to rub off on you. For example, if your friend has financial troubles and instead of coaching her, you just keep loaning her money, and she never pays you back. Now you can't pay your bills, and that friend is nowhere to be found because she has made you financially unstable as well. You let her drag you into her problems.

You become who you hang around with; the decisions your circle enjoys will be the same ones you enjoy. If you never decide to set the standard for your own life and stop following other people's values, don't look to blame anyone when you are at the end of the road and unhappy with how you lived. **I have realized thus far that life is about becoming the best you possible, mastering yourself spiritually, mentally, physically, and emotionally. It takes a lot to understand others; you will never be able to truly care for or understand another person if you never truly understand yourself.**

Allow God to lead you, and follow yourself, toward your goals, your future, and the person you plan to design yourself into. **You get to mold yourself how you want; you are your own replica. You must take responsibility for building it as strongly as possible.**

Chapter Nine:
Follow the LEADER

Everyone has someone they idolize and would want to be like if given the opportunity. **When I say "follow the leader," I don't mean be a follower; I mean be mentored.** Some things you may never grasp on your own if you never get around a person who has done what you want to do. I want to be a great speaker, so I must model, research, and find a mentor who will give me information on being the best. I can speak; most people can, but I need to be able to speak in an educational, informative way to crowds, not just my friends. If you want to become a master, you must find a mentor.

God is the ultimate mentor because He has written everyone's stories, but He does not speak to you how you wish He would; that is why He sends people into your life to help lead you.

Sometimes people stay, and sometimes they leave. It is up to you who you allow to mentor your mind. God does all things to propel you, never to hurt you. All people matter, and all people have a calling. Whom will you allow to be your leader?

In life, doing things alone can be beneficial but has its faults. A mentor is not a "yes man" but an accountability partner. Even if you do things alone when you do not seem sure, you will have this person to go to because you understand that your values are similar, if not the same. It feels good not to always feel like you are the only person feeling something; it feels like having a partner or a twin. Mentors matter and are effective.

I like to give myself mentors I can't touch, such as Eric Thomas and Tony Robbins. These guys have done or are doing what I strive to do. No, I cannot touch them, but I have been to an Eric Thomas conference and seen him live. Eric Thomas embodies the man I hope to be, so I watch and study him in hopes of growing. The difference is that Eric Thomas is a LEADER. He has done what I want to do and motivates me daily on how to get where I want to be. **Everyone needs this person in their lives: a LEADER you can FOLLOW.**

Whether you want to become a better dad, find a dad on social media who is amazing, and follow him. If you want to become a better cook, parent, or friend, find someone who embodies what you see yourself as. I have never seen a problem with seeing myself in other people; that's life. God made no one like you and me; we are unique, but He did create a brain and thinking that allows people to relate in ways we can't always fathom.

Although I have a mentor I cannot touch, I also have one I can. She lives in the same city as me, has the life I want now, and is a call away for help. She has helped me in ways I did not know how to help myself, giving me words of encouragement to take risks I would not have taken on my own. **A mentor will push you in ways you could not push yourself; that is why they lead, and we follow them. A mentor can lead because they won't judge you for where you are and won't let you give up. Most importantly, they will not show you sympathy or empathy when it's not needed.**

My high jump coach in high school was my leader. I followed him and his teachings, and he led me to the state. Robert Kiyosaki, I had always known I was an entrepreneur, but I followed just one of his books, and it led me to opening my own landscaping business. I FOLLOWED THE LEADER. A lot of times, the simplest statements in life can change our entire direction, but as humans, we decide to make it difficult. The right leader for you is a choice made only by you and God, but it is up to you to find out who that is. You cannot think of every idea alone. You may not be able to become that amazing cook alone, but with the right leader, they'll take you places you may have never gone.

I kept getting expelled from middle schools until I reached Hope Prima and met Chelsea Procknow and Ms. Heinen. These two female teachers were leaders I followed regardless of my troubles, and they led me to graduate and move on to high school. If not for their leadership and my willingness to follow, I would have been at an embarrassing age in middle school.

Never let the fact that someone is different from you or is already where you are stop you from allowing them to lead. Ego and pride will stop your fate and destiny. Ego and pride will stop you from meeting people who could have potentially propelled your life. Ego

and pride will not allow you to lead nor be led. A leader who leads with ego and pride will create other leaders that way, and they will only destroy themselves.

If you can never be led, you can never be taught; if you can never be taught, how will you learn and grow? Allow yourself the chip on your shoulder that God only made one of you. You and I have no reason for ego or pride when it comes to leadership because we all want to grow and be taught so we can accelerate our lives and futures. **In order to be led, you must have the will to follow. You must have the WILLPOWER to follow the leader.**

You will know when someone is a leader rather than just being a follower. **A leader is someone who shows you the way to where you desire to go. A leader is NOT someone who gives you the answers so you never learn on your own.** Most people get these things misplaced. The person who gives answers feels powerful because they have valuable information they don't want to share. In clear view, this person is not a leader; they want people to follow them because of what they can do for you, rather than helping you do for yourself.

The mentor you choose should not only be where you want to be; they should have gone through similar situations that you have and will go through. You want to be able to relate to your mentor in ways other than just career interests. In this case, you will be able to learn from them in more ways than one. **Life experience from those who have lived longer than you is some of the best advice you could ingest. Most people dislike the term, but history does repeat itself.**

In order to be ahead of history or at least be prepared, one must go and learn from those who have faced similar problems in the past. **I want you to know from this chapter that it is okay to follow. Who you choose to follow is what I want you to make highly important.** Moses led people away from trouble and into their destinies. Martin Luther King led millions away from hate and into a peaceful future. I compare these two men to help you fathom that the correct LEADER will change your life and give you opportunities you may have never given yourself. Choose wisely.

Chapter Ten:
Your Enemies Are Great Teachers

The purpose of following a leader is so that you can be led to a different place in life. You must realize that more than one person wants what you want, and more than one person might want the same mentor you have. In today's world, wanting what I want makes us competitive; it makes us, in a way, enemies. Even though no human can get in the way of another's blessings because what God has written will happen regardless, the system we live in promotes competition for placement and territory.

Les Brown says, "The journey to success is a constant battle," and he's right.

Not only do we have to battle ourselves, meaning one side of our mind saying we can't while the other says we can, we also have the battle of not letting what others think affect our decisions. Not only do we have enemies who don't want us to succeed before they do, but our biggest enemy is ourselves. **We are someone now that we want to change because the person we are now is not successful.** Read that again. The person you are now eats too much, has no discipline, and is stopping your success. The person you are now will do whatever it takes to keep you the same and not allow you to change. **Your body and mind have adjusted to what you have taught them, and now you have to unteach those things.**

In this phase, your enemies will be your greatest teacher. For example, when turning a bad habit into a good one, your body won't just change easily, but it will change. The enemy is you, complacent, not taking risks, smoking or drinking daily, or striving to put down others while being a bad person yourself. The enemy is YOU. The enemy will give you signs on what it takes to get rid of him. If you are a drug user and stop, you have withdrawals. Withdrawals are the enemy, trying to say, "Come back, you don't really want to change." It will give you aches and pains to test if you have what it takes to actually change. **In this phase, your enemy is fighting your change but also teaching you. The enemy is teaching you what it feels like if you don't change and how much harder it will be next time.**

The more you let the lazy, unmotivated enemy have control, the harder it will be to change physically and mentally. It is an unfortunate fact that if humans do not use certain parts of themselves, they go away. If you do not constantly challenge your brain, you will not learn or grow. If you do not feed yourself, your body won't function. You must get in control of your body and mind and not let them have control of you. The 100 trillion cells in your body are supposed to work for you; you are the boss. These cells are intelligent and memorize what you decide to teach them; your body is a memory bank similar to your brain.

When sickness or cancer arises, that is your body letting you know it is no longer on your side and that you are no longer in control. It does not like how you treated it, so now it is dying and doing its best to treat itself. This is why it is so important to treat your body like a temple.

Otherwise, your body will show you what it is like to lose total control and allow the enemy, the body you don't want, the pain you can't bear, the bad habits you can't let go, to be your ruler. You must tame the enemy and show your body and mind who is in control before it's too late.

It is easy to think negatively; as humans, we are naturally negative due to negativity bias. It takes five positive things to outweigh one negative. What if you didn't see the enemy as just someone to hurt or get out of the way, but as someone sent by God to teach and test you and take you to the next level? If you only see them as a way around and don't learn from them, how will you allow God's plan to go through? Would you rather write your own story? Most people today are writing their own stories, and when they fail, they blame God, the same man who said His story for them includes prosperity and a future.

God told us to lean not on our own understanding for a reason: you and I are flawed and have poor judgment, but God does not. God does nothing on earth without one of His children, and everyone is God's child. If God sent someone you consider an enemy, remember the point is that God sent them and said He would do nothing to harm you but to benefit your future. Open your mind and not your emotions.

Enemies can be some of the greatest teachers if we allow them. **Allow your enemy to show you their flaws, weaknesses, and strengths. Allow them to get vulnerable and out of character, but never allow yourself to do the same. Allow them to use their energy to show you who they are; only then will you defeat them and never be defeated.**

In life, we must perceive things as they are, not as we want them to be. If we do this, we learn to perceive rather than express, which is better in the long run. Most of us express emotions right away because we do not understand; we express ourselves rather than understanding the meaning behind the situation.

One reason your enemy is a teacher is that they dislike you for the things that make you great, qualities they feel they don't have. This teaches you that you have amazing qualities you can continue to develop. Sometimes enemies dislike you for accurate reasons; you have a trait you need to change. It was a great decision for them to point that out, so you can take their anger as a lesson and better yourself. In all times of crisis, there is an opportunity to learn.

Society paints enemies as people to hate, but I say embrace them as you do friends and watch them elevate you. Have the audacity to change yourself and your position and to learn in every moment.

Chapter Eleven:
You Can Leave Willingly or God Will Force You Out

God does everything to benefit His children. God will allow you to walk your own path because He wants you to choose Him willingly, not forcibly, but He will force you out of a situation where you don't belong. **God wants to prosper you, and to do so, He must protect you from choices that do not benefit your life.** For example, you might lose your job unexpectedly. You ask for second chances, but none are given because God does not want them to be. Any situation you are forced out of, even if you didn't want to leave, was God saving you from something that could have potentially ruined you.

God did this for me. I was deeply in love with building an empire and a family with my daughter's mom, and I never took the time to realize who she truly was. I wanted to destroy the family curses where no one was married or stuck it out to reach true happiness. I changed everything about myself to be with her, hanging out less with friends and changing my entire being, while she never had the plans for longevity that I had. I didn't research her history or her past relationships, including the one with her father. I was so driven to make the goal come true that I was blind. She was clearly not into me as much as I was into her. I had changed everything for her; she had changed nothing. I tried to boost her value mentally and physically, but she could never be honest with me.

I probably would never have given up on her if God had not forced me out. We got into a scuffle one day; I did nothing to hurt her horribly, but she called the cops. I had to sit in jail for a day and a half. I had a squeaky-clean record up to this point, which is how I know God forced me out.

God placed me in a position I strived never to be in to show me my daughter's mother was going to ruin me if I did not leave her alone. I had lost myself and forgotten who I was, blinded by my own love.

After I got out of jail, I was placed on a no-contact order. God wanted me to be alone so I could learn and grow without her. It hurt like stepping on a needle, but it needed to happen to keep my successful future intact. **God does everything for a reason: to benefit you and make the story He wrote come true. He knows it all, which is why He wants you to choose Him and follow Him.**

That person may be the love of your moment, but they are not the love of your life; the story God has written is greater. I plead with you to never lean on your own understanding; it will only take you backwards and hurt you. This hurt will affect your body and mind because you believe what you think is the "end-all, be-all," but it never will be.

What God has written will happen, and you can choose to do it the easy way or the hard way. In darkness, God is developing you for the light. You can doubt yourself, but never doubt the creator of your story. Allow God a say so in your life so that nothing has to be forcibly taken away, and everything you give up is genuinely for the best.

Proverbs states that the fool learns from his own mistakes, but the wise man learns from the mistakes of others. God does not like things that can harm you, having control over your life. The man upstairs wants you to live an amazing life, but first, you must give Him control and have faith.

God will also take from you simply because He has something greater in store. It hurts when you lose things without knowing why. For example, you and your best friend have planned since the fifth grade to go to college together, but in your senior year, your friend decides to go to a separate school. This feels like a stab in the back, but change is natural, and it is God's way of asking you to trust Him. Life is about challenges, changes, and faith that God is in control.

God did this in my life with my two best friends from high school, Evan and Jakob. We were brothers; we did everything together, weekends, football, and even betting on our love lives. Jakob was a blessed kid who sold and bought shoes and made me feel like family. I thought we would be a group forever, but God saw otherwise. I wanted to create ownership and a group brand, but Evan and Jakob had other plans. Jakob met a girl and didn't want to talk business as much, and Evan broke his ankle longboarding, which sent our relationship downhill.

Jakob married his girl, and Evan is on the verge of doing the same. Being the outlier who wanted us to chase ownership, I did not respond well; I called them "simps" and said their women had control of them. We barely talk now, and we are no longer brothers. I did not trust God in this instance, but all of that was meant to happen. Jakob is in a happy marriage, Evan is in a wonderful relationship, and I am writing a book. God had them as part of my journey, but He also has journeys for them. How would they reach their greatness if I tried to hold onto them forever? I was being selfish, but God allowed the break so we would all benefit in the end.

Without acknowledging God, you will only lead yourself into ruin and pain. If you aren't happy with your position, the choice of what you do now will change your life forever. Choose wisely.

Chapter Twelve:
Being Alone Will Motivate You in Ways Being Surrounded Never Could

In struggle and pain, most people end up alone. Everyone will go through pain, depression, or anxiety at some point. Being alone can change you if you allow it. Humans naturally hate being alone because they give others the power to make them happy, but in reality, you have complete control of your own happiness.

While being alone, if you evaluate your situation, you realize that it is often where God wants you to be. We spend so much time focusing on others that we never truly understand who we are as individuals. People didn't want to be my friend at a young age because I was truthful and would not lie about my feelings. **I was alone in that notion, but I didn't realize until I was alone often that this made me an outlier.**

Being alone helps you learn about yourself in ways you never would if you were always being told by others who you are. In today's world, humans barely get alone time because society is set up to distract you from your goals and dreams, so you never wonder what the world has to offer. Being alone will elevate your mind and life. If you move away from like-minded people for a summer and return as a different person, you would choose to be alone again rather than go back to where you started.

As soon as you choose YOU over your surroundings, you have an actual chance at changing your life. Being alone will force you to learn what you like and dislike because you are not around others. **You are the technician of your own mind and body; if you never take time to understand your personality, everyone you encounter will be affected negatively by your lack of self-understanding.** It is adamant that every human takes alone time for self-care.

When you are alone, your mind gives you two options: give up and pity yourself, or see it as a chance to get better. Jesus withdrew to solitary places to pray and think, and God knows that alone, you can focus on logical decisions. I am grounded because I have spent a ton of time alone learning my strengths and weaknesses. This mission of life is something you finish alone.

Take time every day to understand yourself. If you never understand yourself, you will never be able to make others understand you. **Be aware of everything that comes with you, even if it takes being lonely for a while. Loneliness can be a gift or a curse, depending on how you choose to deal with it.**

Chapter Thirteen:
Life Is a Gift

The day you were born, God gave you as a gift to your parents with a purpose. God has built multiple gifts inside of you that He has used Himself, and whether we use them is our choice. If you use these gifts as written, you would not know poverty, only the journey to your destiny.

The first gift is **THOUGHT.** God had to think of the wind and water before they became reality, and we can think as well. Our brain is our most powerful gift; we can manifest, meaning our thoughts, through hard work, can become reality. **Use your thoughts wisely and think about what you want so it can be revealed in your life.**

The second gift is **SPEAKING.** God said, "Let there be light," and there was. Our words have power; the things you say to yourself and others are spells. What you believe and say to yourself will play out, whether in a good or bad position; your words and work placed you there. **Be very careful what you say about yourself.**

The third gift is **CHOICE.** God has given you the choice to make a choice, and the biggest one is choosing God to lead your life rather than yourself. Humans choose wrong daily because we think we know everything, and we never do. "Vane" means doing something for a bad reason or to hurt someone, so make your choices wisely, not in vain.

The fourth gift is the **HEART.** God will judge your heart, not your appearance. Human thoughts are more flawed than the heart because we take in information from many sources whose hearts we cannot judge. Your heart should guide you to your destiny. When your heart beats in fear or excitement, it is trying to help you make the right decisions.

The fifth and final gift is **LOVE**, which rules all. God sent Jesus to die for us because He loves us. **Love should lead your heart; the mind can be deceiving. God gave you love so you could forgive, forget, and see change in others.** It is the only thing that will save us in the end. God has also given you a specific gift of greatness inside of you that only you can tap into.

What is your special gift, and will you ever find it?

Chapter Fourteen:
The Gift Only Given to You

God has given each human a specific gift that will benefit them and those they desire to help. The challenge is figuring out what it is. The journey to your destiny is the best part of life because you have no clue which path you need to take. If God showed you everything that would happen, you most likely would not go down that path; instead, He gave you a journey so you would gain faith in Him and your gift.

Stephen Curry developed his gift of shooting, and God did the rest because that was the plan written for him. Greatness is within everyone; those who never reach it are those who never believed they had a gift. **Never blame others for a path only you can walk, or for a blessing you did not receive due to a bad decision. What is meant for you won't miss you.**

Life is hard for most because they are in pursuit of the wrong gift or nothing at all. Everyone has to battle the self they are now to become the self they can be in the future. Doubting your purpose causes anxiety, pain, and stress. **I urge you to pursue things you think you might love with maximum effort. Failure only becomes scary when you decide never to learn from it.** If you do not have a successful life, it is your fault alone, because God gave you a gift, and putting faith into action is your choice.

Your gift will wait for you until death. God wants you to be prosperous and find your gift to benefit the world. **You decide your destiny; God will not force you unless He sees you will be badly hurt. Sometimes, He allows the hurt to build you stronger. No one will have success in your gift the way you will.** Someone may have the same gift, like comedy, but they will never do it as you have done it.

Nipsey Hussle stated he was not in the way of what others were reaching for because no one can get in the way of your purpose but you. **I want you to believe that God has written specifically for you. "Stop**

chasing a high-paying JOB and start discovering your high-paying GIFT." The gift God gave you will pay more than any corporation ever will. The ROI on your gift cannot be calculated. Take responsibility for finding out what is meant for you.

Chapter Fifteen:
The Journey of the Unknown

This is the most important chapter because it is the most overlooked. **The world is filled with people who do not truly know themselves and are told who they are by society.** We do not fully understand our brains, bodies, and souls. The journey of the unknown is the best thing God could have made; if you embrace it, you learn about yourself. **First, you must believe you have a story.**

We gamble or work out because we believe in an outcome; our belief is what pushes us to "just do it." **Believing in the unknown is the opposite of human nature because you have nothing to believe in yet, but you gain belief the further you go.** The journey of the unknown builds us mentally because you have to have a strong mind not to quit, regardless of emotions. It builds us spiritually because we have to have faith that God knows the unknown and is there to prosper us. It builds us emotionally because we must master our emotions or they will master us.

Stress comes from the body and mind not being in alignment. If you tell your mind you want to work out, but your body is used to something else, you will feel sore because it hasn't adjusted. **Once we control our thoughts, we control our bodies.** The journey of the unknown will knock you down to see if you truly want your destiny. If you live a life of struggle and lack of faith, remember you made the choice not to believe God wrote a journey for you.

Walk your journey with "crazy faith." Walk it as a pawn; people think of the pawn as weak, but it is the strongest. If you are strategic and wise on your journey, when you make it to the other side, you can be whatever you want, similar to a pawn becoming a queen or knight. Will you be the pawn thrown off the board, or the one who makes it to your destiny? The choice is yours.

Chapter Sixteen:
Destined to Destroy All Doubt

On my journey, I have tried multiple skills, failing and excelling through them all, but I never gave up. **You must understand you will go through things you do not enjoy, but trying multiple things gives you a greater chance at finding your destiny.** I went from focusing on football to business because I wanted to be an entrepreneur. While in college, I started making music on GarageBand. I was dedicated to it for a year and a half, dropped a song on YouTube, and people started asking about it. I paused because I couldn't afford music videos or equipment, but I never quit; I simply moved on and gained a new skill.

After graduating, I had the mindset that I would rather be broke than work for someone else. I started my landscaping business, but when I had to pay all the bills myself after a breakup, the business went into recovery mode. I loved every second of it because whatever happens in your first business is practice for the second. Then, I started doing Uber Eats so I could work on my own time.

One day, I posted a motivational message from my balcony and felt comfortable speaking to the camera; I named myself "The Doubt Destroyer." I started to post daily content, and it became my passion. I was motivated by Eric Thomas to believe that I could destroy doubt, so I came up with "The Doubt Destroyer" brand. Doubt causes anxiety, shame, envy, and sadness. It causes you to worry about things you have no control over. Doubt causes irritation and anger. I strive to destroy it with love and faith.

If I had never tried music or landscaping, I would have never walked into my destiny as The Doubt Destroyer. **Never stop engaging in new challenges until you find the one that rules your mind. You will know when you find your gift; it will be in your thought process, even in your dreams.** It will be the passion and love you place behind your craft. This journey will not be easy, but never lose faith. Are you the one destined to destroy all doubt?

Chapter Seventeen:
Things Are Not Always as They Seem

Things will happen that you wish never happened because they hurt you, but they were meant to leave your life. We cannot change God's story, and every time we wish we could, we can't. In my experience, even though things hurt, it was best that they happened the way God had written them, and not the way I FELT it should go. My feelings are flawed and unwise; God's are not. **It is all a test of faith. In crisis, lean toward a positive way of thinking to receive the lesson God planned.**

While finishing college and running my business, my grades were falling. One day, my lawnmower started huffing; I put the wrong oil in it and locked the engine. My backup lawnmower then had a wheel snap. I tried renting a lawnmower, but then my edger trimmer wouldn't start. I was using business funds to pay personal bills after my breakup, so I had no money for quick fixes. I paused the business and focused on school. If God had not made my equipment go out, I would have never completely focused on finishing my senior year to become the first graduate.

When you put ultimate trust in God, there is no gray space. It all seems like it is happening badly, but it's working in your favor. In the senior year of high school, two weeks before football camp, I was in a car crash. We were under the influence, and a white car hit us. I flew across the car and woke up in the hospital with a concussion. I had to sit out of summer camp and was devastated. I played the first game without being cleared and played my worst game of the season with a headache.

Months later, I received compensation from the car crash insurance company. This turned out to be positive during a different era of my journey when I was a broke college student. Everything God does has a huge purpose, and the reason for the setback will be revealed. **Things are only as they seem when you lack faith. Pain is guidance; it is your body caring about you and saying it is time for a change.** The only person who will work against you without knowing it is YOU. In all times of challenge, the ultimate destination is GROWTH!

Chapter Eighteen:
What Is Your Destination?

Before you can grow, you must know in what direction your destination is. At least knowing the direction you want to start with is adamant. **No one's destiny is just given to them; they must find it.** You only get one life, but you live every day. Every day is a chance to walk closer to your destiny. It is like a maze set specifically for you. You can allow God to lead through prayer, but you still have to make your earthly decisions. **God's plans are final, which means your destiny is final as well.**

Most never find their destination because they do not believe they have one. Once someone feels they have no destiny, they throw away their life. It is in our nature to enjoy having a destination; it gives life meaning. If you continue to go to a destination that you know is bad for you, it will no longer be growth but recovery.

My daughter's mom and I started our businesses together. She became a lash tech after I encouraged her. She started making new friends at school, and things got rocky. I started taking rides from a girl in my Spanish class, and one day, I called her "pretty eyes" in a text. My MacBook was connected to my phone, and my daughter's mom saw the message while doing homework. The household became toxic; she started leaving for days, so I took her set of house keys, and she left.

We moved into another apartment to build a family, but things got rocky again. I wanted a two-parent household to break the family curse, but she did not. She had trauma from her past that she did not work to change. I thought I could fix her, but all I did was dig myself into a deeper love that she did not feel. We moved out again because we both kept returning to a destination not meant for us.

My grandmother told me God knew I loved her more than she loved me, so He gave me Loyalty, the piece of love from her mom meant for me. Trust God more than yourself. When I finally left that destination, I had to heal from the pain and agony. A destination you won't leave, **even when you know it is wrong,** will only take and take until you are broken. The one percent of people in the world **have** found their gift and their true destination and never looked back.

The greatest teacher you will realize is experience. Try things, hurt yourself, and love yourself on the way to your final destination of prosperity. Walk with urgency, faith, and God. When I moved out, I moved in with my sister and got comfortable procrastinating because I believed I had time. I was saving for a car when my sister was evicted. I had to rush and grab my savings and belongings. This was God saying I must evacuate my plan and let Him lead, He gave me the push to find my own place.

I had also followed the earthly path of gambling my paychecks, and it led nowhere but to more worry. I asked God for discipline, and after praying and choosing to let Him lead, I started saving 70% of my checks. God will always be waiting for you to turn to Him. **If you wait too long, a destination will find you, and you will find yourself complaining to God about something YOU chose.** Choose the right path and the right leader.

Chapter Nineteen:
They Won't Believe (You Must)!

On your journey, people will not believe you can create something or do something that no one else has done before. They could be your parents, siblings, friends, or coaches. You must believe in whatever you seek before it is yours. No one is supposed to believe in your destiny more than you, not even God. Your belief will be the deciding factor. One must think before they act. The belief in what you are thinking is what truly causes action.

The Law of Correspondence states that if you have fear and chaos in your heart, that is what will be revealed in your daily life. What you believe for your health, finances, and relationships will be exactly what your life looks like in reality. After I graduated, I didn't want to work for anyone, but I realized there were more ways to make my dream come true than just my way. I applied for a manager position at Rue21 because I wanted to lead, but I left because I was working more hours on the register than any other employee.

I eventually took a position through my old high school coach. When teachers asked what I did, I told them, "I am building a brand." Some people will stay forever, some are momentary, and some will seek to take you away from your journey. I once bought a $100 ticket to see Eric Thomas in Atlanta after procrastinating; no one else with me believed in or wanted to invest in themselves. It was one of the best decisions I ever made.

If you do not have the firmest belief in yourself, those who see your value will bring you on their path. If you have a talent but do not believe in it, you are easily molded into something else. If you play your music for the first time and someone makes a negative comment, you might start to doubt if you are good. In those times, your belief must be stronger than "theirs."

Confidence is a skill constructed around belief. **Muhammad Ali said he was the greatest before he was.**

What you believe will solidify your position and your life. Fear comes from the devil, while God gives us power, love, and a sound mind. Choosing fear is doubting God and giving the devil power to make you doubt. Use your power of belief to manifest and guide your life. Why do you believe you are here on this earth? Whom do you believe you are meant to be?

Chapter Twenty:
The More You Experience, the More You Have to Offer

Do not hesitate to say "yes" to new experiences. Every person has a different set of experiences because everyone has a different destiny. My experience as a kid going door-to-door hustling gave me the ability to speak with anyone, no matter what culture or walk of life they are from.

Entrepreneurs don't need to know a lot about a little; they need to know a little about a lot.

Never quit on an experience; allow it to play out so you never have to wonder. Mystery lies in almost every new experience, and that gives life meaning. **We fear the unknown because of the "what ifs," but everything was made with a balance of good and bad. Mystery and free will were given to you to give you a CHOICE.**

One of the best experiences of my life was spending a few days in jail. It taught me the superior importance of choice. In jail, you give away your power of choice, and your diet and health are decided for you. The system wants you to realize you do not own your time anymore and seeks to break you mentally. I was locked in a cell with about eight other guys; no one wanted to scare anyone else, everyone just wanted to tell their story.

I talked to a 16-year-old kid with a $30,000 bail who was in for a car chase with guns. I told him God chose him for a reason, and he had to change. Jail made me realize the system teaches time management because you have to find productive things to do with your time. I grabbed a Bible and read every day until I was let out.

The jail experience raised my mental capacity to think and taught me to analyze logically before making any decision. It taught me that TIME is a teacher and a gift.

THE MORE YOU EXPERIENCE, THE MORE YOU HAVE TO OFFER THE WORLD AROUND YOU.

Chapter Twenty-One:
Self-Reflection Will Change You

Sometimes the opinion of others about YOU is correct. You know it's correct because it affects you emotionally and mentally. When you start asking, "Am I this way?" you are self-reflecting. There is a greater you that lies behind all the excuses and bad habits.

In college, I thought my friends Bryce and John were my "real deal brothers," but they began to hang out without me. I looked in the mirror and realized they were jealous, not of my intelligence or football position, but of my looks. They didn't want to bring me to parties because I would take the attention off them. If I hadn't self-reflected, I would have stayed in that toxic environment.

Truth-tellers are often considered crazy, but they are healers. Self-reflection will change you and your environment. No one can self-reflect for you, not even a therapist, who only helps you self-reflect. Opinions create change, but you must allow them to. An opinion can motivate you, or it can push you into a state of delusion where you lie to yourself to make yourself feel better; that is self-pity, not self-reflection.

Michael Jackson said, *"I'm starting with the man in the mirror."*

I now work and coach high jump at the high school I graduated from. Driving the guys home in the school van, I had a moment staring out the same window I did as a student. I realized I was a grown man in the same position waiting for the bus. I had not changed enough to get something I had never had before. Self-reflection brought me peace and allowed me to change my work ethic. Personal development comes after self-reflection. I can guarantee there is something placed within you that is unlike anyone else on this earth.

SELF-REFLECTION WILL CHANGE YOU.

Chapter Twenty-Two:
Your Value Is Already Determined

God has already determined your true value, and no human can place a number on it. If you face your journey with faith that you have a GIFT, no amount of value can be placed on it.

Persistence is the true propeller toward success; it keeps you motivated. You must strengthen your mental state against people who will try to devalue you. If you have a weak mental state, you will allow others to tell you what you are worth.

Once, my cousin and I were mowing a lawn, and the client asked for our price. My cousin said, "$25 or $30, it doesn't matter," but I stopped him and said, "It does matter. We charge $30." He almost allowed someone else to place a value on our work before even seeing it. Never allow any human to determine your value.

When I was a sophomore, my basketball coach wanted me to try out for center even though I had worked on my guard skills. He was sent to the side with centers, and I was livid. I threw my tryout and didn't make the second day. I stood my ground because I knew I was qualified for more. I came back in my senior year and dominated the first two days of tryouts. I scanned the list and saw my name: Pierre McCoy. I had made the varsity team after sitting out two years.

Never let any human negotiate your value when it has been determined by God. Jesus carried His own cross and walked a path of the unknown, and He went to His father for answers. God gave the same unknown journey He is giving you to His own son. **IT HAS ALREADY BEEN DETERMINED.**

Chapter Twenty-Three:
I am Sorry... I Was Wrong... But I am Angry...

I chose to write this chapter to let out the anger I carry.

Ma, I am angry that you took the money I worked hard for as punishment when I was a kid. I am angry that you left my college graduation without taking a picture with me.

Evan, I am angry that we were brothers through car crashes and broken ankles, but now we don't talk because of words. I apologize for trying to stop you from getting into a relationship; I was being selfish.

Pops, I am angry that you only came to my games when I played badly and never when I played well. I am angry that you flex in front of your friends, but you made your own children beg for money. I am angry that you told me you didn't have money for your daughter's bail, but talked the next day about a settlement check coming.

I got vulnerable because I wanted to let go of this anger. I feel like I have lifted a weight off my shoulders by writing it out. I call this book *The Man Before The Millionaire* because I am erasing old values and cleansing myself so that when I do become a millionaire, I will be ready. No one deserves the privilege of seeing your emotions if they do not truly care.

TO *THE MAN BEFORE THE MILLIONAIRE.*

Chapter Twenty-Four:
The Man Before the Millionaire

I am writing this book from the future about things that happened in my past. People ask why I'm writing it before I'm a millionaire, but they don't know my plan. Right now, I am mentally a millionaire. My mind is processing millionaire thoughts and conversations. I desire to change the norm for my family.

My gift is to project my faith and value onto those who think they have none. I am a study hall supervisor, but I understand where I am headed. Every millionaire started with a thought that turned into an idea. **God has given you the gift of speech; you have the power with your words to bring things into existence.**

Money in the hands of the wrong person is evil, but in the hands of the right person, it is a blessing. **I embody a vision to destroy doubt.** Never allow the lack of likes or views to blind you. Post your content, drop your song, and write the book. **Authenticity will take you places that being fake never could.** I have always tried what my family thought to be impossible, and I accomplished it.

So, what about you? Are you willing to take the leap, to trust your own path, and to be bold enough to take a leap towards success? Tell me, are you the one?

Conclusion:
Are You the One?

I was the kid no one wanted to watch, the kid who failed sixth grade and was expelled from three schools. But now I am the first college graduate in my family and the first to chase a dream. I never gave up on anything. **God knew your family would need a leader who would question the comfort zone. It changed my way of thinking; it changed me.** You deserve to become everything people doubted you could be. **ARE YOU THE ONE?**

www.ingramcontent.com/pod-product-compliance
Lightning Source LLC
Chambersburg PA
CBHW041650150726
48005CB00013BA/1601